PUERTO RICO

 Marshall Cavendish
Benchmark

New York

This edition first published in 2011 in
the United States of America by
Marshall Cavendish Benchmark.

Marshall Cavendish Benchmark
99 White Plains Road
Tarrytown, NY 10591
Website: www.marshallcavendish.us

© Marshall Cavendish International (Asia)
Pte Ltd 2011
Originated and designed by Marshall Cavendish
International (Asia) Pte Ltd
A member of Times Publishing Limited
Times Centre, 1 New Industrial Road
Singapore 536196

Written by: Erin Foley
Edited by: Crystal Chan
Designed by: Lock Hong Liang/Steven Tan
Picture research: Thomas Khoo

Library of Congress Cataloging-in-Publication Data
Foley, Erin, 1967-
Puerto Rico / by Erin Foley.
p. cm. -- (Festivals of the world)
Includes bibliographical references and index.
Summary: "This book explores the exciting culture and
many festivals that are celebrated in Puerto Rico"--
Provided by publisher.
ISBN 978-1-60870-105-6
1. Festivals--Puerto Rico--Juvenile literature.
2. Puerto Rico--Social life and customs--
Juvenile literature. I. Title.
GT4828.A2F65 2011
394.26097295--dc22
2010000288
ISBN 978-1-60870-105-6

Printed in Malaysia

1 3 6 5 4 2

Contents

It's Festival Time . . .

The word for festival or party in Spanish is *fiesta* [fee-AYS-tah]. In Puerto Rico, there are many exciting festivals throughout the year. Even some streets in Puerto Rico have their own festivals, and Christmas is celebrated for two months! It's common for feasting, dancing, and partying to go on all night. Puerto Rico is also famous for its music, which is some of the best in the world. So put on a party dress, and follow the music to the plaza. It's festival time in Puerto Rico!

3

Where's Puerto Rico?

Puerto Rico is one of the warm, hilly islands that make up the West Indies. The island faces the Atlantic Ocean to the north, while the sparkling blue Caribbean Sea laps against its southern and eastern coasts. Puerto Rico is the only Spanish colony that never declared its independence, although a few unsuccessful rebellions were attempted. Today it is a commonwealth of the United States. Its people are U.S. citizens, but they cannot vote in presidential elections.

Who Are the Puerto Ricans?

The first people to live in Puerto Rico were the **Taino** people. When the Spanish came to the New World, they forced the Tainos to work for them as slaves. After a short time, there were hardly any Tainos left—they had almost all died from overwork, disease brought by the Europeans, and rebellions. The Spanish then brought in African slaves to work the land. After many years, different peoples and cultures blended together. Today almost all Puerto Ricans have Spanish, African, and native Puerto Rican ancestry. Their culture is also a mixture, however it is strongly

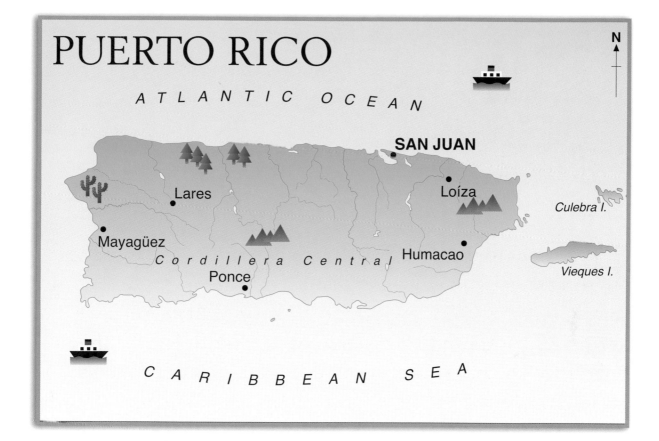

PUERTO RICO

ATLANTIC OCEAN

SAN JUAN

Lares

Loíza

Culebra I.

Mayagüez

C o r d i l l e r a   C e n t r a l

Humacao

Ponce

Vieques I.

CARIBBEAN SEA

N

influenced by their large neighbor to the north, the United States. There are now many Puerto Ricans who live throughout the United States.

✳ There are many old buildings like this one in Puerto Rico. They were built by the Spanish when they ruled the island. This one is in Old San Juan.

What Are the Festivals?

SPRING

* **Emancipation Day**—Celebrates the abolition of slavery.

* **Holy Week and Easter**—Holy Week begins on Palm Sunday when people fill the streets carrying palm fronds to remember Jesus Christ's arrival in Jerusalem. The rest of the week is filled with prayers and reflection before Easter Sunday.

* **Pablo Casals Music Festival**—Classical musicians come from all over the world to perform in the largest musical event in the Caribbean.

Come dance with me for Santiago Apostol!

SUMMER

* **Feast of San Juan Bautista**—At midnight, people walk backward into the ocean to greet St. John the Baptist, patron saint of San Juan and of Puerto Rico.

* **Luis Muñoz Rivera's Birthday**—Celebrates the man who negotiated Puerto Rico's independence from Spain.

* **Commonwealth Constitution Day**—Marks the start of the U.S. invasion of Puerto Rico and celebrates its commonwealth status.

* **Puerto Rican Day**—A grand parade held annually in New York to honor those of Puerto Rican descent.

* **Santiago Apostol**—The colorful festival honoring St. James the Apostle.

AUTUMN

* **Grito de Lares**—One of the most important holidays in Puerto Rico that celebrates the country's independence after the 1868 rebellion.

* **Puerto Rico Day of Discovery**—Celebrates Christopher Columbus's arrival on the island in 1493.

* **Feast of Our Lady of Monserrate**—Pilgrims come to Hormigueros Cathedral to honor Our Lady of Monserrate. They climb the stone stairs of the church on their knees as a sign of respect.

WINTER

* **St. Nicholas Day**—Children look forward to receiving gifts on this day that honors the patron saint of giving.

* **Christmas**—A religious holiday that commemorates the birth of Jesus Christ.

* **Día de los Inocentes**—Also known as The Day of the Innocents, this holiday is a giant carnival with many parades and parties.

* **New Year's Day**—Heralds the start of a new year on the Gregorian calender.

* **Three Kings Day**—The three wise men are remembered on this day for their visit to the infant Jesus Christ and children are given gifts.

* **Octavitas**—People visit one another during this eight-day holiday, so they in turn can receive a visit from their loved ones.

* **Candelaria Day—**Families burn a piece of wood in the community bonfire to protect their house from fire during the year.

* **Calle San Sebastián**—Partygoers wearing colorful masks and costumes take to the streets of Old San Juan to enjoy singing, dancing, and music.

Grab a costume and come celebrate the Día de los Inocentes!

Calle San Sebastián

There are hundreds of festivals in Puerto Rico devoted to **patron saints**. Every town, and even some streets, has its own patron saint and celebrates its saint with a festival. Festivals usually begin about ten days before the actual saint's holiday. The streets of the town fill with stalls selling special foods, and the central plaza fills with music and dancing. There are also games, Ferris wheels, and carousels. People come from miles around to join in the fun. However, the festival is not just for having fun. It is also a time to honor the town's patron saint. On the Sunday closest to the official date, four people carry a wooden image of the saint around the town in a special procession. Mass, or church service, is held twice a day during the festival period.

✳ Musical performances are part of the Calle San Sebastián festival. Puerto Rico is well known for its contributions to classical music, as well as jazz and pop.

Calle San Sebastián

The festival for San Sebastián Street in Old San Juan includes a procession, music, dancing, crafts, and horse shows. The street, known in Spanish as Calle San Sebastián, has a patron saint's day all for itself! The neighborhood becomes choked with people. Bands of musicians march through the streets, strumming Puerto Rican folk music on guitars, or playing dance rhythms with brass horns and drums.

* A parade of musicians marches down Calle San Sebastián.

Horse Shows

Horse shows are a special part of this street fiesta. **Paso Fino** horses have been bred in the Caribbean for a long time, and Puerto Ricans are very proud of them. The name Paso Fino means fine pace. The horse's step is supposed to be so graceful that the rider can carry a full glass of water without spilling a drop.

* Clowns are part of the fun at the Calle San Sebastián festival.

9

Listen to the Music

A big part of Puerto Rican festivals is the music. The most famous kind of Puerto Rican music is **salsa**. Salsa means sauce. Many people eat salsa with Mexican food—it's the spicy sauce that people dip tortilla chips in. Puerto Ricans call this music salsa because it's a blend of styles, like a sauce that has different flavors. Musicians use the percussion sound of traditional Afro-Caribbean music and combine it with the sound of big band jazz, creating a rhythm that makes people want to get up and dance.

Dancing to the Beat

Salsa has become one of the favorite dance rhythms around the world. Some of the most famous salsa musicians include Tito Puente, Gilberto Santa Rosa, Willie Colón, and from Panama, Rubén Blades. A typical band includes a vocalist and chorus, a piano, a bass, a horn section, and a lot of percussion instruments, such as bongos, congas, maracas, timbales, claves, and cowbells.

✳ Music and dance are an extremely important part of Puerto Rican festivals.

THINK ABOUT THIS

Most Puerto Ricans are Catholic, but the influence of the religions of the Taino and West African peoples is evident in Puerto Rican festivals today. Saints' days are a Catholic tradition, but the way they are celebrated is uniquely Puerto Rican.

11

Santiago Apostol

Near the end of July, the coastal town of Loíza fills with a carnival atmosphere. People walk around in fancy costumes with devilish masks. Caribbean rhythms fill the air, and colorful parades occupy the streets. The fiesta for Santiago Apostol [san-tee-AH-go ah-pohs-TOHL], St. James the Apostle, is one of the most colorful festivals in Puerto Rico. It combines traditions of the three cultures that make up Puerto Rico today: African, Spanish, and Taino. Most of the people living in Loíza are descended from African slaves. Over the centuries, this festival has kept alive many of the traditions of the African ancestors of the residents of Loíza. Some of the costumes even reflect Puerto Rico's Taino heritage.

✳ The devil masks worn for the fiesta of Santiago Apostol look very much like the masks made by the African ancestors of today's Puerto Ricans.

Who Is Santiago Apostol?

Many centuries ago, Europeans fought a group of people called the Moors. During a fierce battle, Spanish soldiers believed that they saw Santiago descending from the sky on horseback with sword in hand, in order to help fight the Moors. As a result of this, Santiago became the special saint of Christian soldiers. Later, he was adopted by the army of **conquistadores** [kohn-kees-tah-DOR-ays], or conquerors, who carried their religion to the New World.

✳ The Santiago festival is an occasion to wear traditional Puerto Rican dress.

✳ Performers in elaborate costumes dance outside the cathedral.

Santiago and Shango

In the New World, the Spanish colonists refused to allow the **Yoruba** slaves from West Africa to worship their own god, Shango. Shango was their all-powerful god of thunder, lightning, and war. In images showing the warrior Santiago descending from the clouds, the Africans saw a resemblance to Shango. So they continued to worship Shango, disguised as Santiago. Today, Puerto Rico's Santiago is a mixture of Spanish conquistador and Yoruba war god.

Dancing Along

For nine days before the fiesta for Santiago Apostol, people honor Santiago by gathering to say prayers. On July 25, there is a big procession in which people play music and dance. The procession sways to the sounds of salsa music and traditional *bomba y plena* rhythms. In the bomba y plena, a dancer and a drummer perform a "give and take" of rhythm and dance, while a soloist and chorus sing along. This dance, which blends African and Hispanic styles, started in the coastal town of Ponce. It is a uniquely Puerto Rican tradition.

✳ The bomba y plena is a special Puerto Rican invention that combines Spanish and African styles to make something totally new.

Wild Costumes

There is one part of the festival called "The Devils Against the Christians," in which the battle between the Spanish and the Moors is reenacted. People dress in fancy costumes with masks and painted faces. Some wear brightly colored clothes and white masks. They are the Spanish *caballeros* [cah-bah-YAY-rohs], or men on horseback. Others dress as **vejigantes** [vay-hee-GAHN-tays] to represent the Moors. They wear devilish masks made from painted coconut shells with long horns along the top or sides. Some men dress as clowns or as crazy women, called *locas*. The locas blacken their faces, wear mismatched clothes, and often act silly or pretend to sweep the streets and porches as they go along.

✳ The masks worn by vejigantes are often very large, colorful, and frightening.

15

Las Navidades

During the Christmas season, or *las Navidades* [lahs nah-vee-DAH-days], Puerto Ricans have a huge celebration. Relatives and friends arrive from the United States, laden with gifts and good wishes for residents of *la Isla* [lah EES-lah], as Puerto Ricans fondly call their homeland.

Putting Up Lights

The Christmas season officially begins on St. Nicholas Day, which is celebrated on December 15. People prepare for the holiday season by putting up beautifully detailed nativity scenes, Christmas trees, and colored lights. Nativity scenes are a Puerto Rican tradition. Sometimes they are very elaborate. Christmas trees are a more recent addition.

Christmas lights are also a big part of a Puerto Rican Christmas. People decorate their houses, front yards, windows, and balconies with impressive displays of lights that shine all night long. Sometimes whole neighborhoods join together to create elaborate holiday decorations.

* Left: Santa Claus is not native to Puerto Rico, but he has become popular as a result of the United States' influence.

* Opposite: Christmas mass at the Cathedral of San Juan Bautista.

* The Christmas feast includes roast pig. Early in the day, the pig is placed over an open pit. It is turned on a spit over the fire for several hours until it is fully cooked and the skin is crunchy. Every part of the pig is eaten, including the knuckles and the feet.

Cuatro Groups

The traditional music of Puerto Rico is performed by *cuatro* groups. These groups take their name from the cuatro, a small Puerto Rican guitar with four strings. It used to be a tradition for small bands of musicians to travel from town to town throughout the holiday season, singing folksongs. They still play at the early morning masses celebrated during the nine days before Christmas eve.

* You might see a cuatro group singing and playing as they stroll down the street at Christmastime.

✳ Parrandas may start with a handful of people and continue until the whole town has joined in.

Waking Up the Neighbors

An old Puerto Rican tradition is the *parranda* [pah-RHAN-dah], in which a small group of people gathers to visit friends and to sing to them. The special holiday songs they sing celebrate Christmas, family, and good times. The parranda musicians sing loudly and even bang on pots and pans for extra noise. Revelers also surprise their friends with *asaltos* [ah-SAL-tohs], an unexpected form of the parranda. They do this by waking up their friends late at night and demanding to be let into the house, where they are given food and drink. After singing together, they try to persuade their friends to join them in surprising others. As the night wears on, the group grows larger, noisier, and merrier. The traveling party may continue until all hours of the morning.

Around Christmas

Christmas is a highlight of the Puerto Rican year. In fact, Puerto Ricans like Christmas so much that they don't want it to end, so they go on celebrating right through to January 15! The season is filled with celebrations of different parts of the Christmas story. Each of these celebrations has its own traditions.

Los Inocentes

On December 28, after Christmas has just ended, it's time for another festival! This is the *Día de los Inocentes* [DEE-ah day lohs ee-noh-SAIN-tays], the Day of the Innocents. In the biblical story, King Herod wanted to get rid of the Christ child, so he ordered that all male children under two years old be killed. This festival honors the memory of the children who died during that time.

* For Día de los Inocentes, people dress up in costumes like this that cover them up completely.

Kidnapping the Boys

Día de los Inocentes is like a big carnival. The traditional celebration involved men dressing up as Herod's soldiers and going from house to house. At each house, they would "kidnap" the oldest boy from the family. To get their children back, the families would offer the soldiers gifts. When the boys were returned to their homes, people celebrated with a big party. Today Día de los Inocentes is more like April Fool's Day. People play tricks on each other, or try to fool one another into believing stories that are not true.

Party Time in Hatillo

The little town of Hatillo has an especially big celebration for Día de los Inocentes. The whole town takes part in a big parade. Everyone gets dressed up in costumes and masks. Afterward, there's a big party in the public square. This celebration was brought to Puerto Rico by people from the Canary Islands who had settled there.

＊ Climbing a slippery, greased pole is another tradition for Día de los Inocentes.

＊ Parades are usually held as part of the celebrations for Día de los Inocentes.

Three Kings Day

On January 6, Catholics celebrate the arrival of the Magi, or three kings, at the manger of the baby Jesus. Wooden statues of the three kings are put up in front of the capitol building in San Juan. Older Puerto Ricans may still gather at a neighbor's house to pray together and to honor the three wise men, but today this is a holiday for children. Traditionally, Three Kings Day was the day when Catholics received presents. Although many people have adopted the American custom of exchanging gifts on Christmas, most still have a few gifts to open on January 6.

✴ Wooden figures of the three kings.

Grass for the Camels

The night before Three Kings Day, children gather fresh grass and place it in shoe boxes under their beds for the kings' camels. It is thought that the kings rode camels to visit Jesus. Children believe that the Magi reward good children by replacing the grass with gifts. Their parents might also put out a few sweets for the wise men. The children wake up in the morning and excitedly check the boxes to find out what the kings have left for them. They might also find their shoes filled with special gifts. Then the children quickly dress and go out to watch or join the procession. Children in San Juan flock to the old fortress, El Morro, to collect free candy and toys.

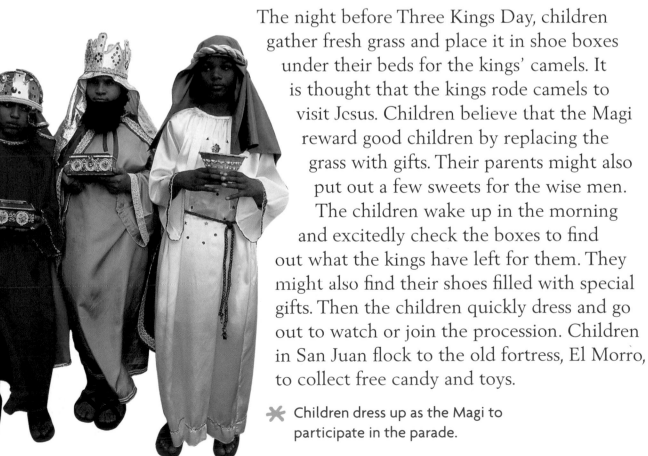

✴ Children dress up as the Magi to participate in the parade.

Las Octavitas

Many people prolong las Navidades beyond Three Kings Day for the eight days of adoration of the baby Jesus, called *las Octavitas* [lahs oak-tah-VEE-tahs]. During this time, parents and godparents exchange visits, sing, and recite prayers—and continue with more parties, eating, and drinking. It is a tradition that if a person receives a visit from a friend or relative on Three Kings Day, that person is supposed to return the visit eight days later. The word *Octavitas* means little eights, meaning eight days after January 6.

THINK ABOUT THIS

Puerto Ricans borrow ideas for festivals from all over the world. Many ideas for masks and music came from West Africa. Some dances and costumes came from Spain. Even the Canary Islands contributed to the celebration of Día de los Inocentes!

✳ Men dressed as the three kings of Juan Díaz Village arrive at San Jose de Caguas Church.

Patriotic Festivals

The Taino people who first lived in Puerto Rico called their island *Boriquén* [boh-ree-KAIN]. Today Puerto Ricans often refer to themselves as *Boricuas* [boh-REE-kwas]. Although Puerto Rico has never been an independent country, there is much patriotic feeling among Puerto Ricans both on the island and in the United States. Many people would like to see an independent Puerto Rico. Others just want to celebrate their homeland and its traditions. There are many occasions, both in Puerto Rico and in the United States, for Puerto Ricans to show off their pride and their hope for the future.

✱ A statue of Ramón Betances, who inspired the Grito de Lares rebellion.

Shout for Freedom

On the night of September 23, 1868, a group of rebels marched into Lares. They took over the town and arrested the mayor. The next morning, they declared the independence of Puerto Rico. The rebellion later failed, but it was the closest Puerto Rico came to being its own country. On September 24, the small town of Lares celebrates the *Grito de Lares* [GREE-toh day LAH-rays] as the birth of Puerto Rico's independence from Spain.

New York Goes Boricua

There are many Puerto Ricans in the United States, and many live in New York City. Many Puerto Ricans in the United States have never lived in Puerto Rico, but they are still proud of being Puerto Rican. In New York City, the second Sunday in June is Puerto Rican Day. The day explodes with parades, banners, and dancers marching in time to a Caribbean rhythm. In 2006, more than 80,000 participants marched in the parade and nearly two million spectators lined the parade route.

✳ New Yorkers celebrate Puerto Rican Day with a big parade.

Things for You to Do

The *coquí* [ko-KEE] is a little tree frog that is found only in Puerto Rico. Its song can be heard at night all over Puerto Rico, and it has become a favorite symbol of the island. The song of the coquí is the only natural song that is a perfect seventh, a special musical combination. Maybe the unusual musical talent of the coquí has had an effect on Puerto Ricans. Puerto Rico has produced music that is famous all over the world. Listen to the coquí for inspiration, make some maracas, and add a little music of your own to your fiesta!

Make Some Maracas

Maracas are a kind of rattle usually made from a gourd that is carved and stained for decoration and then mounted on a stick. You can also make maracas out of papier-mâché. Blow up a small balloon. Cover it with a few layers of papier-mâché and let it dry. Then pop the balloon. Put some beans or seeds inside to create a nice sound. Then put a stick in the hole to make a handle and seal it with masking tape. When it's dry, paint your maracas in bright colors. Now you're ready to play!

Percussion Galore

Puerto Ricans are great inventors of musical instruments. They developed three different kinds of guitar—with three, four, or six strings. Puerto Ricans especially enjoy percussion instruments, such as the *güiro* [GWEE-roh], a notched gourd played by drawing a stick across it. This instrument originally came from the Tainos people. A hollowed tree trunk beaten with sticks also comes from the Tainos, as do maracas. Many Puerto Ricans are talented musicians and are able to play several instruments. In many families, it's a talent that has been passed down from generation to generation.

FURTHER INFORMATION

Books: *Puerto Rico.* Howard Gutner (Children's Press, 2009).

Puerto Rico in American History. Richard Worth (Enslow Publishers, Inc., 2008).

Shake It, Morena!: And Other Folklore from Puerto Rico. Compiled by Carmen T. Bernier-Grand (Millbrook Press, 2006).

A Visit to Puerto Rico. Leila Merrell Foster (Heinemann Library, 2008).

Websites: www.elboricua.com/BoricuaKids.html—Puerto Rico's history made easy with bite-sized facts.

www.gotopuertorico.com/puerto-rico-attractions.php—Contains a list of top attractions to explore and experience in Puerto Rico.

www.timeforkids.com/TFK/teachers/aw/wr/main/0,28132,702661,00.html—Learn more about the U.S. Commonwealth of Puerto Rico in this site just for young readers.

Make a Vejigante Mask

Puerto Rican mask makers usually use a coconut shell to make vejigante masks, but you can also make one using papiermâché. Then you'll be ready to join in the fun at Loíza for the feast of Santiago Apostol.

You will need:

1. Two pieces of cardboard 11 1/2 inches x 14 inches (29 x 35 cm)
2. Poster paints
3. A medium paintbrush
4. A small paintbrush
5. Strips of newspaper
6. 3–4 tablespoons of flour
7. Scissors
8. Stapler
9. Masking tape

28

1 Cut a cardboard circle 10 inches (25 cm) across. At the bottom of the circle, make a cut 3 1/2 inches (9 cm) long. Toward the top, make two diagonal cuts about 2 inches (5 cm) long.

2 Overlap the edges of the lower cut and staple. Overlap the edges of the top cuts and staple. Stir the flour into 2 cups (480 ml) of warm water, making a thin paste. Dip the strips of paper in the flour paste and apply to the mask. Cover the mask with two or three layers of papier-mâché. Let dry.

3 Cut the second piece of cardboard in half lengthwise. Roll each piece into a long, narrow cone, and secure it with tape. Cover with several layers of papier-mâché.

4 Ask an adult to help you cut out eyes and a mouth. Make small cuts in the base of the horns. Papier-mâché the horns to the mask, adding several layers. Let dry.

5 Paint your mask in bright colors. Vejigante masks are usually green, red, orange, yellow, purple, and black, often with dots painted on them. If you'd like, attach a piece of string or elastic to the back of the mask so that it will stay on. Try not to frighten anyone with your mask!

Make Besitos de Coco

These chewy little cookies are called *besitos de coco* [bay-SEE-tohs day KOH-koh], which means coconut kisses. Try them, and they'll be sure to make your fiesta extra special!

You will need:

1. 3 cups (225 g) of coconut flakes
2. 1/2 cup (70 g) flour
3. 4 egg yolks
4. 1 cup (200 g) brown sugar
5. 1/4 teaspoon salt
6. 1/4 cup (50 g) butter, softened
7. 1/2 teaspoon vanilla
8. Pastry brush
9. Spatula
10. Wooden spoon
11. Measuring spoons
12. Measuring cups
13. Large bowl
14. Baking tray
15. Pot holder

1 With clean hands, measure all the ingredients into a large bowl and mix them together using the wooden spoon.

2 Pick up a spoonful of the batter and roll it into a ball. Continue until you've used up all the batter. You should have about twenty-four balls.

3 Grease a baking tray with butter. With an adult's help, preheat the oven to 350°F (180°C).

4 Spread the balls out on the greased baking tray. Put them in the oven. Be very careful, and be sure to use a pot holder (ask an adult to help you with this). Bake them for 30–40 minutes until they're golden brown.

Glossary

asalto	A surprise gathering of musicians and friends.
bomba y plena	A dance that combines African and Spanish elements.
Boricua	A popular name that Puerto Ricans call themselves.
Boriquén	Original Taino name for Puerto Rico.
conquistador	Conqueror; name for Spanish conquerors of the New World.
cuatro	A small guitar, or groups playing traditional music.
la Isla	Name for Puerto Rico used by Puerto Ricans living in the United States.
parranda	A group of people singing Christmas carols.
Paso Fino	A type of Puerto Rican horse.
patron saint	A saint who is dedicated to the care of a town.
salsa	Music that combines jazz with Afro-Caribbean percussion.
Taino	The original inhabitants of Puerto Rico.
vejigantes	Masqueraders who wear devil masks for festivals.
Yoruba	A West African group who were ancestors of many Puerto Ricans.

Index

Photo Credits
Alamy/Photolibrary: cover, 1, 7, 13 (top), 15, 17, 18 (both), 21 (bottom), 24 (bottom), 28; Chip & Rosa Maria Peterson: 3, 24 (top); Corbis: 2, 4, 6, 14 (bottom), 23, 27 (top); David Simson: 25 (top); Getty Images: 10, 11, 13 (bottom); Hutchison Library: 20; Joe Colon, Puerto Rico Tourism Co.: 12; Manny Patino: 19, 21 (top); Photolibrary: 5, 8, 9 (both), 14 (top), 22 (top), 25 (bottom); Suzanne Murphy/ ddbstock: 16, 22 (bottom)